THE SPIRIT SAID 'GROW'

This book may be kept

Vinson Synan

INNOVATIONS
IN MISSION

Bryant L. Myers, Series Editor

G. H. Cachiaras Memorial Library
920 Mayowood Road SW
Rochester, Minnesota 55902

MARC

THE SPIRIT SAID "GROW"
The astounding worldwide expansion of Pentecostal and
charismatic churches.

by Vinson Synan

This book is comprised of material from a lecture series titled
"Evangelization and the Charismatic Renewal" given at the
1990 Church Growth Lectureship at the School of World
Mission, Fuller Theological Seminary, Pasadena, CA

Published by MARC, A division of World Vision
International, 919 West Huntington Drive, Monrovia, CA
91016, U.S.A.

Printed in the United States of America. Cover design: Edler
Graphics, Monrovia, California. Typography: Palatino 14 pts,
reduced photographically to 82%

ISBN: 0-912552-73-5

The Spirit Said "Grow" is the fourth in MARC's Innovations in Mission series.

Other books in this series:

The Nonresidential Missionary
Facing the Powers
Empowering the Poor

CONTENTS

FOREWORD

I SPENT THE FIRST 20 YEARS OF MY LIFE as an anti-Pentecostal —
not just "non," but "anti." I was taught that the "bizarre" gifts of
the Spirit, such as tongues, healing, and prophecy had ceased
with the apostolic age. My Bible was the Scofield Bible and
B.B. Warfield was one of my theological heroes.

The person who helped to broaden my vision more than
anyone else was Donald McGavran, father of the church
growth movement. He showed me in the late 1960's that if I
wanted to understand church growth, I should study the most
vigorously growing churches I could find. I was a missionary
in Latin America at the time, and though I found it a bit unset-
tling, it was becoming clear to me that by far the fastest growing churches in Latin America were Pentecostal churches.

The more I studied the Pentecostals, the more fascinated
I became. My fascination soon turned into genuine appreciation, and appreciation led to a degree of participation. I have
never quite become a Pentecostal, but I certainly enjoy them
and am blessed by being with them.

I wrote a book in 1973 on my findings titled *Look Out!
The Pentecostals Are Coming!* (Creation House). Later I updated
it and changed the title to *Spiritual Power and Church Growth*
(Creation House). Few of my friends were ready to read that
back in the mid-1970's. Contrary to my intentions, more Pentecostals read the book than the non-Pentecostal evangelicals.

How the world has changed! Vinson Synan, by consensus the ranking historian in the Pentecostal-charismatic movement, has shown us that indeed, the Pentecostals have come.
The Spirit Said "Grow" brings us up to date. It is a book that has

long been needed.

Synan is dealing with a unique historical phenomenon. My research has led me to make this bold statement:

> *In all of human history, no other non-political, non-militaristic, voluntary human movement has grown as rapidly as the Pentecostal-charismatic movement in the last 25 years.*

While many have come to recognize this as part of contemporary Christian reality, Vinson Synan is unique in providing a clear, concise summary of this phenomenon.

I had the privilege of hearing my good friend Vinson deliver these lectures live at Fuller. Students and faculty alike were enthralled with the stimulating presentation and the array of facts, figures, events and personalities he assembled. I rejoice the material is now available to all.

Synan frequently cites expert statistician David Barrett throughout this book. However, with or without the help of Barrett, any careful observer visiting churches internationally would know for certain that the considerable majority of committed Christians worldwide would be regarded as part of the Pentecostal-charismatic stream. How this amazing situation came about is the exciting story of this book.

C. Peter Wagner
Fuller Theological Seminary
Pasadena, California
May 1992

A word for today

BECAUSE OF ITS BRIEF HISTORY and incredible growth rates, the appearance of the Pentecostal-charismatic movement may well be the single most important fact of twentieth century Christianity.

I must admit that I have a hard time realizing that my wife's grandmother, born in 1898 and still going strong, has lived throughout the entire span of Pentecostal history. When she was born, the category, as we now know it, did not even exist. Now (1990) there are 193 million members of the Pentecostal family — by far the largest such Protestant group in the world.

It is also appropriate here to focus on evangelization. The 1990 Church Growth lectures at Fuller Theological Seminary, which constitute the substance of this book, were titled "Evangelization and the Charismatic Renewal." Today, and to me, nothing is more important.

For the past five years, I have chaired the North American Renewal Service Committee and have been involved in the leadership of three national conferences under the banner "Congress on the Holy Spirit and World Evangelization." Evangelism thus has been the theme of my ministry. I can honestly say that I have never seen such a universal consensus among Pentecostals and charismatics around this focus. From practically every quarter, magazine articles, conferences and subconferences dedicated to the theme of world evangelization support this impression.

In Indianapolis in August (1990), about 25,000 of us gathered in the Hoosier Dome under the theme, "Evangelize

the World Now!" The leaders of over 50 Pentecostal denominations, charismatic renewal movements, independent ministries and fellowships confirmed and emphasized the theme
in morning denominational sessions, afternoon "Schools of
Evangelism," and in the huge plenary rallies.

Of course, the classical Pentecostals, being birthed
among evangelicals, have always been evangelistic and mis-
sion-minded. But the charismatic renewal movements have
sometimes seemed to be more interested in the rejuvenation of
their denominations than in doing primary evangelizing.
Now, these movements are squarely behind the cause of
world evangelization. Some are even organizing sending
agencies. One of these, the "Order of St. Philip the Evangelist,"
established by Episcopal charismatics, will soon be sending
out itinerant lay evangelists around the world to engage in
"tentmaking" ministries to unreached peoples.

The non-denominational charismatics are also entering
into the quest with new zeal and vision. The 1989 publication
by Strang Communications of David Shibley's book, *A Force in
the Earth*, sounds an evangelistic call and symbolizes a new
wave of world outreach which could add millions of converts
to the kingdom of Christ.

Across the board, there is a new understanding of how
the gifts of the Spirit can and must be used to evangelize the
lost, and not only to edify those already in the church. The
prominence given to signs and wonders as tools of evangelization is adding new appreciation for the possibilities inherent in
the power of the Holy Spirit to win the world for Christ.

More and more, I tend to measure any teaching or
movement on the basis of the evangelistic results that follow
it. To me, the ultimate test of any movement is its success in
evangelization. I am applying that test more and more in my
travel and research.

For purposes of defining this theme, I am using the term
"charismatic" in this book in its broadest sense. Thus I will
deal with classical Pentecostals, charismatic renewalists, and
"third wavers" — all of them — as being in some sense charismatics who are interested in renewal and the expansion of the

kingdom throughout the world.

People frequently ask me, "What is God doing now? What is the word that the Spirit is saying to the churches today? What is the 'now word' to this generation?" For five years I have been answering "EVANGELIZE" — or in another word, "GROW," remembering that the first and third letters spell "GO!"

This is what the Spirit is saying to the churches. Evangelization and the charismatic movement are inseparably linked by the Author and Enabler of the Christian mission.

Vinson Synan

ONE

A global family: size and scope of the movement

THE YEAR 1980, AS I SEE IT, was a watershed year in the history of Christianity, and particularly of the charismatic movement.

In that year, David Barrett finished the basic research for his monumental *World Christian Encyclopedia* (Oxford University Press, 1982), which was to appear in print two years later. Barrett's findings indicated some major changes in the Christian world. Among them:

- The number of non-white Christians surpassed the number of white Christians for the first time in history.

- The Pentecostals surpassed all other groups of Protestants to become the largest Protestant family in the world.

To me, that was news. At that time the Pentecostals numbered 51 million, while the Anglicans and Baptists were close behind with about 50 million apiece. Incredible news indeed, in view of the fact that Pentecostalism was then barely eighty years old, while the churches of the Reformation era had over 400 years of history behind them. To me, this was fantastic — it excited me.

I shall never forget the galvanizing effect of reading the *Time* magazine review of Barrett's book. It kindled in me an overwhelming desire to learn just who all these Pentecostals were, and where they lived. As a person born and reared in the parsonage of a Pentecostal preacher, this was — and to me still remains — a fact of utmost fascination and importance. I felt I just had to get acquainted with David Barrett and learn more about his research.

That opportunity came in 1985, when I met Barrett in Richmond, Virginia, where he was working for the Southern Baptist Foreign Missions Board. I immediately encouraged him to produce an authoritative survey of the world Pentecostal-charismatic family which would serve as a base index from which to gauge the future growth and development of the movements.

At the same time, Peter Wagner was doing similar research in Pasadena, while Stanley Burgess, Gary McGee and Patrick Alexander were working on the *Dictionary of Pentecostal and Charismatic Movements*. The publication of this award-winning book by Zondervan in 1988 coincided with the appearance in *The International Bulletin of Missionary Research* of a study by Barrett entitled "A Survey of the Pentecostal-Charismatic Movements with their goal of World Evangelization." These publications made 1988 also a landmark year.

Barrett's survey revealed the tremendous global growth of the Pentecostal-charismatic movement in this century. In addition to this, the survey pointed out the great variety of groupings connected with this trend. In doing so, Barrett introduced some new words to the ecclesiastical lexicon, such as "pre-Pentecostals," "quasi-Pentecostals," "Third Wavers," "crypto-charismatics," and "post-charismatics." Although we will deal with some of these categories in greater detail later, I would like at this point to give some basic definitions which will clarify the ensuing discussion.

Pre-Pentecostals

These include many persons and movements prior to the twentieth century which could be considered antecedents of the modern Pentecostal movements. They would include:

a. Monks, priests, brothers and sisters in Catholic, Orthodox, or Anglican churches who exercised spiritual gifts over the centuries.

b. Mormons, Quakers, Shakers and other similar sects outside the mainline churches.

c. Nineteenth century Holiness and social reform movements such as the "sanctified Methodists," the Holiness churches springing from Methodism, and the "Higher Life" movements with roots in the Keswick conferences.

Non-white, indigenous quasi-Pentecostals

These are "quasi" ("apparently-seemingly-largely") Pentecostal movements indigenous to Christians in non-white races across the world who are phenomenologically Pentecostal (dreams, visions, filling with the Spirit, tongues, prophecies, healing through prayer, expressive worship and praise, etc.). These were begun without Western mission board support. Barrett places their beginnings in 1741 in the Caribbean region.

Black-non-white, indigenous Pentecostals

These groups are related to the classical Pentecostals, but are not supported or controlled by Western (white) churches. This category would include the 3,700,000 members of the American Church of God in Christ, or the 3,000,000 plus members of the South African Zionist Church, which annually convenes the largest gathering of Christians in the world (3 million) in their Easter conferences in Pietermaritzburg, South Africa.

Holiness-Pentecostals

These are the original American Pentecostals who came from the Methodist perfectionist tradition. Represented by Charles Fox Parham, the formulator of Pentecostal theology (1901), and William J. Seymour, pastor of the Azusa Street Mission (1906), this category included the first denominations to declare a Pentecostal position. They taught a three-stage deeper life experience — of justification, sanctification and baptism in the Holy Spirit, evidenced by speaking in other tongues. Among these were the Church of God (Cleveland, TN), the Pentecostal Holiness Church and the Church of God in Christ.

Baptistic Pentecostals

This was the second wave of American Pentecostalism, espousing a two-stage teaching on the baptism in the Holy Spirit. It was known as the "Finished Work" movement, as taught by theologian William Durham. Churches of this style included the Assemblies of God, founded in 1914, the International Church of the Foursquare Gospel and most of the Pentecostal denominations in the world founded after 1914.

Oneness Pentecostals

Beginning in 1915 as a theological controversy in the infant Assemblies of God, the "Oneness" (or often called "Jesus Only") movement included such churches as the Pentecostal Assemblies of the World, the United Pentecostal Church and several churches using variations of the term "apostolic" in their name. Unitarian Pentecostals are the only Pentecostals who say one must speak with tongues to be saved.

Protestant charismatics

Known first as "neo-Pentecostals," this stream began about 1960 with the ministry of Episcopal priest Dennis Bennett in Van Nuys, California. Although Bennett and many of the first neo-Pentecostals accepted the "initial evidence" theory, many others saw tongues as only one of many gifts that come with the baptism of the Holy Spirit. Bennett's groundbreaking success in remaining in his denomination opened the way for thousands of other ministers and laymen to begin charismatic "renewal" movements within their own churches.

Catholic charismatics

Beginning at DuQuesne University in 1967 and spreading rapidly around the world, this movement finally proved the universality of Pentecostalism and opened the door for massive Catholic charismatic renewal movements in over 100 nations. They, along with most Protestant charismatics, spoke of the Pentecostal experience as a "release" of the Holy Spirit, bringing with it tongues as the usual consequence and also releasing other gifts of the Spirit.

Third Wavers

Beginning about 1980, these are mainline evangelicals who exercise spiritual gifts and emphasize signs and wonders, but who do not identify with either the Pentecostal or charismatic movements. This tendency may have started in California, in John Wimber's classes at Fuller Seminary. Third Wavers do not teach a crisis experience of baptism in the Holy Spirit, and they see tongues as only one of the many gifts of the Spirit.

Crypto-charismatics

This category refers to individuals who exercise spiritual gifts but who, because of persecution or peril to their ecclesiastic standing, keep their experience a secret. They also include Spirit-filled Christians in non-Christian nations where the practice of Christianity is forbidden.

Post-charismatics

These are persons, both Catholic and Protestant, who have been baptized in the Holy Spirit and have experienced spiritual gifts, but for a variety of reasons, do not currently attend weekly or monthly charismatic meetings.

With these definitions firmly in mind, let us return to the Barrett survey. His *World Christian Encyclopedia* data became the basis for the updated statistics which were reproduced in 1990 by the Lausanne II Statistical Task Force, of which I was a member. To provide a context for the data about Pentecostals-charismatics on page 11, I am submitting the chart at the top of the next page.

This chart shows the size of the movement as compared with other religions and Christian groupings. The total number of Pentecostal-charismatics was estimated at 372,651,000, as of July, 1990. By 1992, the total had passed the 410 million mark.

When it comes specifically to the Pentecostal-charismatics, it can be seen that the growth has come in successive "waves." Somewhat to my surprise, Barrett accepted the "Third Wave" theory proposed by Peter Wagner in 1983, which divided the movements into three categories, described

---

MAJOR RELIGIONS IN 1990

of World* Religions (in million)

Christian	1,759
Muslim	935
Hindu	705
Buddhist	323
Jewish	18

of Christians (in million)

Roman Catholics	962
Pentecostal—charismatics	372
Evangelicals	295
Eastern Orthodox	179

of Protestants

Denominational Pentecostals	193,689,000
Anglicans (Episcopalians)	53,820,000
Baptists	53,500,000
Lutherans	50,797,000
Presbyterians	45,800,000
Methodists	30,415,000

*World Population................5,292 million

---

as:

1. *Pentecostalism* (the classical Pentecostals from 1901),

2. *The charismatic movement* (1960: Protestant; 1967: Catholic) and

3. *Third Wave renewal* (ca. 1980).

These categories are expanded and detailed in the chart at the top of the next page.

Within these categories exist a tremendous variety of groups, all of which believe that the Holy Spirit still manifests the charismata in modern times. They exist in 11,000 Pentecostal and 3,000 independent charismatic denomina-

Pre-Pentecostals (Holiness) 5,400,000
Denominational Pentecostals...........................193,689,000
Chinese Pentecostals 50,000,000

Mainline Charismatics 140,572,050
Protestant Charismatics 55,322,050
    Active Protestant Charismatics 23,722,050
    Post-charismatic Protestants..................31,600,000
Catholic Charismatics 72,063,000
    Active Catholic Charismatics.................11,813,000
    Post-charismatic Catholics 60,250,000

Mainline Thirdwavers..33,000,000

World Total of Pentecostal—charismatics in 1990.............372,651,000

World Percentage of Pentecostal—charismatic Christians 21.4%

tions, as well as in all the 150 major non-Pentecostal families of Christian churches. They are to be found in no less than 230 nations of the world.

Of these Pentecostals and charismatics, 29 percent are white and 71 percent non-white. The newest and most exciting variety are the Chinese "house-church" Pentecostals, of whom an estimated 50 million existed in 1990.

In all, Pentecostal-charismatics are growing at a rate of 19 million per year, or at least 54,000 per day, totaling in 1990 21.4 percent of the world's Christians. And this "explosive, uncontrollable growth" continues, according to Barrett, despite the fact that these are the "most harassed, persecuted, suffering and martyred" Christians in recent history.

It is obvious that in any analysis of church growth around the world, the Pentecostal-charismatic family cannot be overlooked. By God's grace, it is a twentieth century phenomenon to gladden the heart of every Christian.

TWO

A closer look; what the family is like

DESPITE SOMETIMES FURIOUS OPPOSITION, the Pentecostal-charismatic movement has prospered. The annual personal income of this huge company of believers surpassed one trillion dollars in 1990, of which $37 billion was given to Christian causes.

Another astounding fact that emerged from the Barrett-Lausanne studies is that fully one fourth of all full-time Christian workers in the world are from the Pentecostal-charismatic persuasion. They reached a grand total of 1,100,000 (out of an estimated 4,000,000 in 1990).

In spite of these astonishing facts, there are some sobering statistics which should concern every leader of this movement. Of all the billions of dollars earned by these earnest believers, only fifteen cents per week per person is given to the cause of world evangelization. Imagine what the record would be if each member gave only $1.00 per week.

Another problem for the movement is the "enormous turnover" among Pentecostals and charismatics, leading Barrett to create a new category which he labels "post-charismatics." These are people who have once been active in the renewal, but have dropped out for various reasons. Although many of these are serving in the churches in full-time ministries but are not able to attend regular charismatic meetings, many others have drifted back into inactivity and indifference. These people, who have been called the "graduates" or "alumni" of the movement, numbered no less than 91 million in 1990.

The overall picture drawn by Barrett, however, is one of

dynamic growth. Although the Pentecostal category did not even exist prior to 1901, Pentecostals now number almost four times the size of the next largest Protestant denominational family. By comparing the charts in chapter one, Barrett's estimates for the major Protestant families in 1990 are as follows:

Denominational Pentecostals	193,689,000
Anglicans (Episcopalians)	53,820,000
Baptists	53,500,000
Lutherans	50,797,000
Presbyterians	45,800,000
Methodists	30,415,000

The year 1990 was also an epochal year because the denominational Pentecostals surpassed the combined membership of Eastern Orthodox churches as the second largest denominational family on earth — second only to the Roman Catholic church. The figures for these three persuasions are as follows:

Roman Catholics	962,000,000
Denominational Pentecostals	193,000,000
Eastern Orthodox	179,000,000

The emergence of "super-churches"

This growth pattern can also be seen in the mushrooming surge of Pentecostal "super-churches" over the last two decades.

I became interested in the super-church phenomenon in 1966 when I made my first trip to Chile and saw firsthand the size and scope of the Chilean Pentecostal movement. To give perspective, at that time the First Baptist Church of Dallas, pastored by W. A. Criswell, was said to be the largest Baptist church in the world with some 20,000 members. I discovered, however, that at the same time, the Jotabeche Methodist Pentecostal Church in Santiago, pastored by Javier Vasquez, claimed 40,000 members. Simultaneously, in Seoul, Korea, Pastor Yonggi Cho was approaching 10,000 members in his tent church.

When I reported in *Christianity Today* that Vasquez' church might be the world's largest congregation, I was met with some skepticism and ridicule, especially from my fellow Pentecostals. This became more pronounced as the Jotabeche church climbed to 60,000 and then to 100,000 members. But by 1980, Pastor Cho's congregation in Seoul grew so rapidly that it surpassed Vasquez' church, making the latter the world's second largest congregation. With Cho in 1990 claiming 800,000 members, and Vasquez 350,000, few people now question the 40,000 claim made by the Jotabeche church in 1967.

In Manila in 1989, I asked Peter Wagner what his most recent figures were concerning the largest congregations in the Protestant world. His answer is found in the following chart:

FIVE LARGEST CHURCHES IN THE WORLD

Full Gospel Assembly......................................800,000
    Seoul, Korea
    Paul Yonggi Cho, pastor

Jotabeche Methodist Pentecostal............................350,000
    Santiago, Chile
    Javier Vasquez, pastor

Vision del Futuro.......................................145,000
    Buenos Aires, Argentina
    Omar Cabrera, pastor

Brazil Para Cristo...85,000
    Sao Paulo, Brazil
    Manuel de Mello, pastor

Deeper Christian Life Ministry.................................65,000
    Lagos, Nigeria
    William Kumuyi, pastor

A similar, but different, listing of the mega-churches

appeared in *The Christian World Almanac,* published in Wheaton, IL, by Tyndale House Books in 1990. It was prepared by Dr. John Vaughan, and the discrepancies that can be seen between it and the Peter Wagner listing are no doubt attributable to divergent definitions of "church" and "congregation." It shows the size of the ten largest churches, as shown in the following chart:

WORLD'S 10 LARGEST CHURCHES (1989-1990)[1]

Sunday Worship Attend.	*Church*	*Pastor*
180,000	**Yoido Full Gospel Church** Seoul, Korea	Paul Yonggi Cho
80,000	**Vision del Futuro** Santa Fe, Argentina	Omar Cabrera
70,000	**Deeper Christian Life Ministry** Akoka, Yaba: Lagos, Nigeria	William Kumuyi
70,000	**Waves of Love and Peace** Buenos Aires, Argentina	Hector Jimenez
50,000	**Jotabeche Methodist Pentecostal** Santiago, Chile	Javier Vasquez
50,000	**Kum Ran Methodist Church** Seoul, Korea	Hong Do Kim
47,000	**Nambu Full Gospel Church** Seoul, Korea	Yong Mok Cho
40,000	**Soong Eui Methodist Church** Inchon, Korea	Ho Moon Lee
35,000	**Jesus is Lord Fellowship** Manila, Philippines	Eddie Villanueva
30,000	**Madureira Assembly of God** Rio de Janerio, Brazil	Francisco Fonto

---

1   Draper, Edythe, ed., *The Almanac of the Christian World,* Tyndale House Publishers Inc., 1990, pp 367-368.

Since I visited Pastor Kumuyi's church in March (1990), I have found that some of his provincial congregations count from 8,000 to 10,000 members.

I have also been told personally by Yonggi Cho that his younger brother in Seoul, Yong Mok Cho, pastors a church, the Nambu Full Gospel Church, with over 200,000 members. It started eight years ago when Cho "gave" his brother 5,000 members to plant a new church. At present, it is not listed as one of the largest churches, although I hope to visit it soon in order to document its size and impact.

As examples of the success of the Pentecostal-charismatic movements in evangelizing the world, I will cite three current cases which have recently come to my attention.

The mass crusades in Africa of Reinhard Bonnke

Probably the most successful mass evangelist in history is Reinhard Bonnke, the German Pentecostal evangelist who regularly ministers to crowds of 100,000 or more in his African crusades.

He recently purchased an amplifier system with which he can address over 1,500,000 persons at one time. In October, 1990, he used the new system for the first time in a crusade in Kaduna, Nigeria, which turned out to be his largest and most successful crusade to date. In six services, 1,670,000 persons attended, with the final crowd numbering over 500,000 in Kaduna's downtown Muhammad Murtala square. More than 150,000 decision cards were signed by new converts and distributed to the pastors of 255 local churches which sponsored the crusade.

Kaduna is a Muslim city where as recently as 1987, nineteen Christians were martyred and many Christian churches burned. The crusade was held there, nevertheless, and miracles of healing were a major attraction which drew people from all religions and levels of society.

Bonnke confidently expects in the near future to address crowds of over one million at a time, and even believes that he will live to see one million converted in a single crusade. This he calls the "combine harvest" era of reaping souls. His slogans are "plundering hell to populate heaven," and "Africa shall be saved."

The media blitz campaigns of CBN

Early in 1990, the Christian Broadcasting Network, under the leadership of Pat Robertson, conducted a crusade in Central America called "Project Light." Described as a "multi-media blitz," the project was conducted in El Salvador and Guatemala and was sponsored by most of the evangelical and Pentecostal churches of the two nations.

The "media blitz" included newspaper stories and advertisements, billboards, 8,500,000 pieces of literature, showings of the "Jesus film" in outlying rural areas, telephone counselors, "Operation Blessing" — food for the needy, distributed by local churches — and three successive nights of prime-time TV specials.

The television specials broke all previous viewing records in both countries. A follow-up program was carried out by 20,000 counselors from sponsoring churches. At the end of the blitz, professional pollsters and door-to-door surveyors estimated that more than two million people were led to Christ in one month.

The "World Census Crusades" of the Happy Hunters

Another innovative evangelistic method is the "Census" technique planned by Charles and Frances Hunter (the "Happy Hunters") in Honduras. In the summer of 1990, the Hunters made plans to organize a census of the entire nation of Honduras, which was to have been completed in January, 1991.

The census takers not only were to take the names and addresses of the interviewees, but also were to witness to the gospel and leave a Bible in every household in the nation (500,000). Based on a trial run in 1990, the Hunters believed that over two million persons would be converted in the census period. A follow-up rally in Tegucigalpa was planned for January, where 200,000 attendants were expected in the stadium.

The Hunters claim that "God said 'take a census of the world.'" They are also making plans to evangelize America by leading "twenty to thirty million Christians starting at a given signal to evangelize the United States and finish the census in one week." They believe that "not since the resurrection of Jesus have there been such shock waves ringing through hell since God said 'take a census of the world.'"

These and other examples show that the Pentecostals and charismatics are not lacking in imagination and vision as they enter the decade of the 1990's. Indeed, whether or not these techniques bear as much fruit as intended, these developments indicate that a new level of evangelization may be breaking loose in the world, mostly led by Pentecostals and charismatics. I personally believe that the 1990's will show unprecedented evangelization and church growth unparalleled since the early days of the apostolic church.

The eminent historian, David Edwin Harrell, says in *Pentecostals from the Inside Out*:

> *In short, the Pentecostal-charismatic movement in the United States that began as a gushing stream in the early twentieth century has now broadened into a broad and imposing river. For all of its swiftness at the end of the 1980's, the flow has slowed somewhat, and one can hardly see from one bank of the river to the other.*
>
> *But this expansive river continues to overflow its banks. Both inside and outside the United States, the current still spills into narrow rivulets, surging and rolling to receptive crevices in virgin lands. More and more, those new streams are fed by their own wells of the Spirit, but most owe their beginnings to the great river of American Pentecostalism.*

THREE

False starts and failures

Afterward he appeared to the eleven themselves as they sat at table; and he upbraided them for their unbelief and hardness of heart, because they had not believed those who saw him after he had risen. And he said to them, "Go into all the world and preach the gospel to the whole creation. He who believes and is baptized will be saved; but he who does not believe will be condemned. And these signs will accompany those who believe: in my name they will cast out demons; they will speak in new tongues; they will pick up serpents, and if they drink any deadly thing, it will not hurt them; they will lay their hands on the sick, and they will recover."

So then the Lord Jesus, after he had spoken to them, was taken up into heaven, and sat down at the right hand of God. And they went forth and preached everywhere, while the Lord worked with them and confirmed the message by the signs that attended it. Amen. (Mark 16:14-20 RSV)

THIS PASSAGE TIES WORLD EVANGELIZATION TO the manifestation of the charismata with signs and wonders following. Despite the problems with the text, it indicates, at least, that from the earliest times, signs and wonders were associated with carrying out the Great Commission.

Since the ascension of Christ, there have been at least 700 systematic plans to evangelize the world. Most have failed, and are now defunct. Of course, the original master plan was a charismatic one, as announced in Acts 1:8: "But you shall receive power when the Holy Spirit has come upon you; and you shall be my witnesses in Jerusalem and in all Judea and Samaria and to the end of the earth."

In Matthew 21:29, the unfaithful son said, "I go, sir," but did not go into the harvest. Much the same can be said of the church through the centuries. We have said, "I go, sir," to the Lord, but now — 66 generations after the Resurrection — only one third of the world knows the name of Jesus as Lord, while 25 percent of the population has never heard the gospel even once.

A birds-eye view of world evangelization efforts

The following timetable suggests the sad record of the church over the centuries:

By A.D. 200   Origen proclaimed that the task was already completed.

By A.D. 300   Chrysostom realized that the task was still incomplete.

A.D. 1000   The Slavs were evangelized under Saints Methodius and Cyril.

Post-1492   The Spanish and Portuguese "converted" 20 million Amerindians; proposed the conversion of China by military force.

Pre -1900   John R. Mott called for world evangelization in 25 years, "during this generation."

1918   A plan was proposed in which virtually all U.S. Christians (except Roman Catholics and Southern Baptists), including 34 denominations, cooperated. By 1920 it had collapsed because the churches refused to give money.

1961   Billy Graham challenged the church to "evangelize the world in one decade." Failed.

1972	"Project Look-up" proposed to use satellites in orbit. Failed.
1974	"Bold Mission" was proposed by the Southern Baptists to reach the whole world by A.D. 2000. Still in process.
1984	Charismatic plan initiated, involving all denominations, to make the majority of the world Christian by the year A.D. 2000. In process.

Why have the foregoing plans largely failed? The church either said, "I go, sir," but did not go, or it went forth without the full power of the Holy Spirit.

Specific charismatic movements that failed

Because of the tremendous record of growth among Pentecostals and charismatics in the twentieth century, some people think that growth is automatic if the charismata are manifested. This, of course, is a mistake, since there have been many movements marked by the use of the gifts which failed, in fact, to grow.

I would like now to look at several charismatic-type movements in church history which failed to grow; some of which turned to heresy; and indeed, some of which disappeared from the earth completely.

Montanism

In many ways, Montanism resembles the modern Pentecostal-charismatic renewal movements of the twentieth century. Begun in the remote rural region of Phrygia in Asia Minor, its social and economic roots were similar to those of the classical Pentecostals. As is the case with many modern Pentecostals, the Montanists were ascetic, rigorous, charismatic and chiliastic (i.e. anticipating the millennium of Christ's reign on earth).

In about A.D. 160, the sect was founded and led by Montanus, a convert to Christianity, who attracted two "prophetesses," Prisca and Maximilla. With him, they led the movement.

It is generally agreed that Montanism grew out of a deep disillusionment with the increasing moral laxity in the church. Considerable license was being granted to the masses of new converts by a church which was anxious to accommodate newcomers without compelling them to live by as strict a moral code as was required of the religious and clergy. The rigorous asceticism of Montanism attracted many to its cause, including the illustrious Tertullian of North Africa, a region where the movement flourished.

As a holiness persuasion, Montanism forbade second marriages, instituted strict rules for fasting and encouraged members to face martyrdom without attempting to escape. Tertullian himself was so taken with the movement that he labeled mainstream Catholics "psychics" or "animal men," while calling the Montanists "pneumatics," or "Spirit filled." Tertullian and other Montanists were such perfectionists that they refused infant baptism on the grounds that if a church member sinned after baptism, he had committed the unpardonable sin, for which there was no possibility of restoration or forgiveness.

Not only was Montanism a holiness movement, it was a charismatic and prophetic movement as well. Calling itself "the new prophecy," it emphasized enthusiastic worship, ecstatic utterances (generally recognized as glossolalia), and prophetic messages addressed to the entire church. The special source of Montanist prophecy was held to be the Holy Spirit, or the Paraclete. Montanus spoke of the Paraclete as saying, "Behold, the man is as a lyre, and I sweep over him as a plectrum."

Montanus' style of prophecy, as described by Eusebius (an opponent), was as follows:

> He became beside himself, and being suddenly in a frenzy and ecstasy, he raved, and began to babble strange things, prophesying in a manner contrary to the constant custom of the church which had been handed down by tradition from the beginning. (Ecc. Hist. Vol. 5:16, p. 7: Schaff ed.)

The major burden of Montanist prophecy was the soon return of Christ, an imminent event which would end the persecutions of the righteous and usher in the final judgment. The principal problem with the "Nova Profetia" was that Montanus seemed to refuse to accept the closing of the canon and placed his own prophecies on the level of the already accepted Scriptures. The fact that he was a peasant with no education or high episcopal rank also flew in the face of the already advanced tendency of the bishops to preempt prophetic and other charismatic gifts, combining them with the mundane authority of the episcopacy.

Despite the support of Tertullian and a determined effort to remain within the church, Montanism was ultimately condemned by the Synod of Iconium about A.D. 230 when the church refused to accept Montanist baptisms. Thereafter, the Montanist movement went underground and lasted a few more centuries before disappearing altogether.

Montanism thus failed to win the church to its views, and with its condemnation came the final closing of the canon of Scripture as well as a legacy of deep suspicion towards all enthusiastic and prophetic movements that were to come in the ensuing centuries.

Although Montanism was condemned, it was never convicted of heresy. Many of the monstrous charges of immorality leveled against Montanus and the prophetesses have been largely discounted by modern scholarship. Recent Roman Catholic scholars, such as Kilian McDonnell, now believe that the Catholic church "over-reacted" to Montanism, with the result that the special gifts were allowed gradually to die out in the church, giving place to a "cessation of the charismata" theory, first enunciated by St. Augustine.

Perhaps the reasons for the failure of the movement lay in its excessive judgmentalism and legalism, its attempts to place the new prophecies on the level of the Scriptures, and in its incapacity to win enough powerful bishops to its cause.

Shakerism

Another charismatic group which has practically disappeared was commonly known as the "Shakers," or, more properly, "The United Society of Believers in Christ's Second Appearing," or simply "The Millennial Church." As these names imply, the Shakers were a chiliastic society which expected the soon return of Christ in its day. As such, its members considered themselves to be the "Church of the Last Dispensation."

Shakerism grew out of a Quaker revival in Manchester, England, in 1747, which was led by some French "prophets" who had immigrated to England. Converts in this meeting were James and Jane Wardley and Ann Lee who not only quaked under the Spirit, but shook in ecstasy, earning them the unusual sobriquet of "shaking Quakers," or simply "Shakers." Because of these physical manifestations, they were persecuted and at times imprisoned.

Ann Lee soon rose to be the head of the sect and imposed her visionary standards on the group. Married to a blacksmith in 1760, she suffered the death of four infants through miscarriages, after which she declared celibacy to be the ultimate evidence of holiness in this life. In 1770 she received a vision of Jesus Christ which became the basis of the Shaker societies. After this she was generally called "Mother Ann."

Her teachings included virginal purity, Christian communism and a total separation from the world. In addition, Lee held that God is a "duality" rather than a trinity, with Jesus being the "male" and Ann Lee the "female" elements of the Godhead. Worship was held in "meeting houses" featuring singing and dancing before the Lord. Speaking and singing in tongues was encouraged, with Lee even putting her glossolalia songs into print.

In 1774, Ann Lee and five followers came to America as the result of a prophecy. In the new world, they hoped for more freedom than they had experienced in England. By 1776 they had established themselves in New York where, despite persecutions, they were able to recruit several Baptists to their cause.

After Lee's death in 1784, she was succeeded by James Whittaker, who began organizing Shaker communities centered around "meeting houses" for worship. The headquarters community was built in Mt. Lebanon, New York, from which point the Shakers spread to other parts of the United States. In a few years, eighteen Shaker communities were established in New England, Ohio and Kentucky. At their height, these societies claimed almost 6,000 members in America.

In order to join a community, one had to progress through three "orders" of affiliation, the last of which conferred full membership in the society. Celibacy was required for all members, even for those already married. These couples and others were forced to live in dormitories with the men and women separated by a wide hall. Those who were unmarried took a lifetime vow of celibacy. Much of the liturgy of "dancing in the Spirit" involved members "shaking off" lustful desires of the flesh.

Of course, it was difficult to evangelize new members into the community, with many new converts coming from among the misfits, or orphans who were befriended by the members. Naturally, there were no nurseries for infants or Sunday school classes for the children, since none were produced by the members. One could not speak, therefore, of "biological growth" within the movement.

The communitarian emphasis of Shakerism called people from the world to live a separated life within the walls of the communities. These were largely self-sufficient economies with almost every necessity met by what was produced on the premises. They are more famous now for their music and furniture than for their religious notions.

Although Shakers spoke in tongues and prophesied, they had practically disappeared by 1950. At the last count, about three Shakers were left, each an elderly woman in her nineties. The communities, like the one in Shakertown, Kentucky, are beautiful museums of an earlier economy and piety.

While the Shakers were undeniably charismatic, they were also theological heretics and social hermits. They never intended to evangelize the world. They were rather a sect awaiting the end of the age while fighting off the evil desires of the flesh.

Any evaluation today becomes an epitaph.

FOUR

Not in sharp focus

LIKE THE MONTANISTS WHO PRECEDED THEM, the Shakers are now past history. However, other more contemporary manifestations of renewal have contributed, albeit sometimes only slightly, to the present current of growth. Perhaps a matter of timing, or of doctrinal deficiency — some factor of history or of theology — has jarred them out of focus. But their significance in the Pentecostal-charismatic movement cannot, nevertheless, be overlooked.

Irvingism (Catholic Apostolic Church)

An acknowledged precursor of the modern Pentecostal persuasion was another nineteenth century movement inaugurated by Presbyterian pastor Edward Irving in London, and known to history as the "Catholic Apostolic Church." Some writers, such as Earnest Sandeen, place the roots of this movement, as well as that of modern fundamentalism and Pentecostalism, in the period following the French Revolution. The overthrow of the Pope in 1798 sparked an interest in prophecy which profoundly affected Protestantism for the next century.

In the 1820's, a group of Bible students had formed around a wealthy English banker, Henry Drummond, to search for signs of the times which pointed to the second coming of Christ. Some of the leaders in the circle were Lewis Way, an American, and John Nelson Darby, founder of the Plymouth Brethren. By 1825, Edward Irving had not only joined the group and absorbed its teachings, but had predicted that the second coming of Christ would occur in 1864. He also taught that since the five-fold offices of apostles, prophets, evangelists, pastors and teachers had disappeared from the church, the Holy Ghost had deserted it.

Irving soon became the national leader of the Drummond group, due to his immense fame and popularity as the leading preacher in London. By 1830, his Presbyterian church on Regent Square was attracting crowds of 2,000 to hear his flowery rhetorical sermons. A tall man with long black hair, Irving was described as having an overpowering personality.

Convinced that the church was near to experiencing the second coming of Christ, Irving and his friends searched the Scriptures for signs of the imminent event. They discovered three signs in particular:

1. the return of the Jews to Palestine;

2. the restoration of the five-fold ministries to the church;

3. the reappearance of the charismata through a general outpouring of the Holy Spirit.

From 1828 to 1830, Irving and others made trips to Scotland looking for those rumored to be prophesying and speaking in tongues. By March, 1830, the search was ended when a group near Glasgow, led by a Mary Campbell, spoke in tongues to the approval of a commission from London which accepted them as genuine signs of the last days. As word spread that the charismata had been restored, examples of speech in tongues occurred in Anglican, Presbyterian and dissenter churches in London.

The reception by the London churches was less than enthusiastic, however, with an Anglican bishop and several dissenting churches forbidding the practice. The one church that encouraged tongues and prophecy in regular services was Irving's large and influential Presbyterian congregation at Regent Square.

In October, 1831, Mary Campbell was allowed to speak in tongues and prophesy on Sunday morning in Irving's church, creating scenes of confusion and consternation among the members. The major messages uttered were, "Behold the Bridegroom cometh. Go ye out to meet him," and "the body of Christ, the body of Christ."

In a short time, the Presbytery investigated Irving, conducted a trial and dismissed him from the ministry. He was convicted, however, more for his Christology than for his charismatic leanings. After this, Irving led 800 followers in organizing an independent congregation where the gifts of the Spirit would be welcomed.

In the next year, 1832, Irving's circle of followers created a college of twelve modern-day "apostles." These were appointed "by the Spirit" and were to be the last-days counterpart of the original twelve apostles. They were to be the last testimony before the rapture of the church.

Led by a prominent lawyer, J. B. Carsdale, this group included eight Anglicans, three Presbyterians and one dissenter. Notably absent was Irving himself, who was recognized only as the "angel" (pastor) of his local church. The twelve apostles were socially prominent Englishmen, including lawyers, country gentlemen, members of Parliament and, of course, clergymen. In a short time, seven churches were organized in London, corresponding to the seven churches in Asia Minor.

Through travels and reading, the apostles soon developed elaborate rituals and liturgies drawn from Roman Catholic and Protestant, as well as Eastern Orthodox sources. Prophecies were uttered, recorded and treasured as "words from the Lord," binding on all Christians. The robes and eucharistic celebrations showed a remarkable Catholic influence. The name chosen for the group was "Catholic Apostolic Church," although critics often referred to its adherents simply as "Irvingites." In 1834, Irving died in Scotland, a sad figure who never spoke in tongues or shared in the apostleship of the church he had inspired.

Although as many as 80 churches were started in England, and missions were begun in Holland, Germany and the United States, the Catholic Apostolic Church never flourished. And in England it practically disappeared soon after the turn of the century. The last of the English apostles died in 1901 — interestingly, the same year that Pentecostalism broke out in the United States. Since Christ was soon to return, the twelve apostles decreed that no successors to them were to be named. Only in Germany and Holland, where apostolic successors were consecrated, did the church survive.

Called the "New Apostolics," the movement with apostolic successors thrives today in Holland, Germany, South Africa (110,000 members in 1,000 churches) and the United States, where in 1990 there were 36,972 members in 491 congregations. In Germany the Neuapostolische Kirche had 330,000 adult members in 2,900 churches, governed by 48 apostles in 1980 — the third largest denomination in Germany.

Since all baptized Christians of all other churches were considered also to be members of the Catholic Apostolic Church, personal evangelism was not encouraged. The major evangelistic thrust of the apostles was to issue "Testimonies" to the ruling powers of England and the major European powers. Thus in 1836, Apostle Spencer Percival read aloud a lengthy testimony to King William IV and members of his Privy Council. It was said that "the King was moved to tears."

The Testimony, 27 single-spaced pages long, was a surprisingly political document, supporting all the Tory causes of the day. It denounced the Reform Bill of 1832, the granting of seats in Parliament to Jews and "Papists," and all efforts to grant more democracy to the middle class, much less to the poor who owned no property. Not surprisingly, it strongly defended the divine right of kings to rule in the name of Jesus Christ.

Declaring that the British government was "at an end," the apostles predicted "judgment," "anarchy" and "desolation" to Great Britain unless everyone, from the king on down, should repent. It ended with these words: "The testimony of the Lord your God against the land — the warning of His judgments — and the message of His mercy."

Similar testimonies were sent to the archbishops and bishops of the United Church of England and Ireland as well as to the "rulers in church and state in all Christian lands."

In the meantime, the church took steps to control prophecy among its members. After the publication of Carsdale's *Prophesying and the Ministry of the Prophet in the Christian*

Church in 1868, prophecy and tongues practically ceased among them.

In retrospect, the downfall of the Catholic Apostolic Church in Great Britain seems to have been in its preoccupation with the theoretical aspects of the restoration of charisms and apostolic offices rather than in sending missionaries and evangelists to win the poor and unreached peoples of the world. It was essentially an aristocratic and intellectual restorationist movement with almost undisguised contempt for the impoverished and unevangelized nations around the globe.

The Apostolic Faith (Baxter Springs, Kansas)

In the very period which saw the decline and fall of the Catholic Apostolic Church in England, which ended for all practical purposes in 1901 with the death of its last British apostle, the American Pentecostal movement had its beginnings in Topeka, Kansas. On January 1, 1901, Agnes Ozman spoke in tongues at Charles Parham's College of Bethel, in a building known locally as "Stone's Folly." Interestingly enough, this building was constructed in the style of an English country manor, not dissimilar to the Drummond Estate at Albury. Another superficial link with its English antecedents was Parham's choice of a name for his new movement, "Apostolic Faith."

Although Parham and his students attracted wide attention in the churches and press, the movement he sparked never became widespread until after the advent of the Azusa Street revival in Los Angeles 1906 under the black preacher William J. Seymour.

Meanwhile, Parham and his followers conducted whirlwind revivals in the South and Middle West from 1901 to 1906 with much fanfare and controversy. His most successful meetings came in 1906 in Zion, Illinois, where no less than 500 ministers were won to the new Pentecostal cause. Some have estimated that Parham had attracted some 25,000 followers by 1906 when Azusa Street took over the spiritual leadership of Pentecostalism.

The main reason why Parham's Apostolic Faith Church never prospered was his dogmatic opposition to any kind of church organization. This position, along with his refusal to take offerings for the support of his work, caused many of his talented followers to join other Pentecostal churches which were later founded and well organized to plant churches and send missionaries around the world. Many of Parhams's followers ultimately established the Assemblies of God in 1914, which became the major missionary church of the Pentecostal-charismatic movement.

By 1990, the original "Apostolic Faith" churches founded by Parham numbered no more than 30 small congregations, centering around the denomination's headquarters in Baxter Springs, Kansas. But the broader movement which he started, the worldwide Pentecostal movement, numbered no less than 193 million people around the world by 1990.

The Apostolic Faith Mission (Portland, Oregon)

A movement that split off from Azusa Street was founded by Florence Crawford in 1907 in Portland, Oregon. Crawford was able to begin on a large scale because she took with her the mailing list for Seymour's nationally influential magazine, *Apostolic Faith*. Like Parham and Seymour, she called her movement "The Apostolic Faith."

Crawford's movement failed to grow for several reasons. Firstly, it was under female leadership, and the Pentecostal world had not yet sorted out its position on the ordination of women. Secondly, Crawford taught one of the strictest versions ever devised of the holiness lifestyle code. Her most controversial position was that no member of her church, lay or clergy, could ever remarry after divorce, regardless of the guilt or innocence of either party.

Adhering strictly to the second-work theory of sanctification, as taught by Parham and Seymour, Crawford insisted on a strict code of outward holiness in dress, especially for women. Like Parham, she refused to take offerings for the support of her mission. Any group that compromised on these points was "disfellowshipped" from her movement.

After 1909, when the designation "Pentecostal" gained popular usage among tongues-speakers, her followers stoutly refused to use the label, thus distancing them from the broader movement. By 1990, the Apostolic Faith (Portland, Oregon) numbered only 45 churches around the world with some 4,500 members.

Although Crawford's movement never thrived in the United States, it did experience growth overseas. In a short time, the church had far more members in Africa than in its country of origin. Its major contribution to church growth was the fact that William Kumuyi of Nigeria was converted in an Apostolic Faith Mission congregation.

When Kumuyi desired to minister with signs and wonders, however, he was ejected from the church, forcing him to form his own denomination which he called the "Deeper Life Ministry." By 1990, Kumuyi had established a mother church in Lagos with 70,000 members, and could count as well some 350,000 believers throughout Nigeria in over 2,000 congregations. He also was sending missionaries to thirty different African nations. These churches could be considered a spin-off of the Apostolic Faith Mission of Florence Crawford.

Alexander Boddy (England)

Alexander Boddy led the first British Pentecostal renewal movement in 1907 after receiving the Pentecostal tongues experience during a visit by Thomas Ball Barratt. For many years, Boddy was the rector of the Anglican parish in the city of Sunderland, England. He, along with his congregation and family, experienced a full-blown charismatic renewal immediately after Barratt's visit. Active for many years in the Keswick movement, Boddy was sure that the holiness and higher life movements in Britain were ready for the new Pentecostal message.

In the 1907 Keswick convention, he printed and distributed a flyer to the delegates entitled, "A New Pentecost for England?" By and large, however, the Keswick following rejected Boddy's call for evidential tongues and ignored his efforts to promote a charismatic renewal. Undaunted, Boddy published from 1908 to 1926 a Pentecostal magazine called *Confidence*. Through the ministry of Boddy and his gifted wife Mary, hundreds of persons received the baptism in the Holy Spirit in the Whitsuntide (Pentecost) conferences which he conducted in Sunderland from 1908 to 1914.

Although England had to wait until after 1960 for the full arrival of the charismatic renewal, Boddy planted seed that flourished after his death. His most famous convert, Smith Wigglesworth, was to bear a tremendous influence in his worldwide ministry in later years. Michael Harper has stated that Boddy was "a man ahead of his times." This seems to be the key. Boddy was ready, but Britain was not.

Jonathan Paul (Germany)

Another European Pentecostal movement that experienced great opposition and little growth was the German group founded by the German Holiness preacher Jonathan Paul in 1907. The early Pentecostals in Germany exhibited most of the emotional and charismatic manifestations that were common in the rest of the world. In Germany, however, with the deeply ingrained anti-Schwarmerei tradition dating from the time of Luther, Paul met with stern resistance.

In 1909, the famous "Berlin Declaration" was published by a group of German evangelicals. It stated that tongues were "not from above, but from below." This helped to place the Pentecostals under a cloud of suspicion by Lutheran and Roman Catholic Church authorities. As a result, the growth of Pentecostalism in Germany was painfully slow.

Paul's own church, the Mulheim Association of Christian Fellowships, numbered only 14,000 adult members in 1980, according to David Barrett, while the largest and most successful German Pentecostal Movement, the Bund Frier Pfingstgemeinden (BFP) numbered only some 20,000 members in 253 churches in 1980.

The German Pentecostal movement, although existing under extreme negative pressure from the mainline churches, nevertheless produced the most important mass evangelist of the 1980's, Reinhard Bonnke. As a traditional missionary in

South Africa from 1967 to 1974, he experienced minimal success until he entered into a signs and wonders ministry in 1975 in Botswana.

Thereafter, his crusades attracted such crowds that in 1983 he purchased a crusade tent which seated no less than 34,000. By 1989, however, his crowds, which often numbered over 100,000, forced him to abandon the tent for open air meetings. His organization, called "Christ for All Nations" ministered under the slogan "Africa shall be saved."

In a sense, the seed planted by Jonathan Paul in Germany in 1907, bore tremendous fruit in Africa in the 1980's.

FIVE

Missionaries of the one-way ticket

THUS FAR WE HAVE LOOKED AT SEVERAL SEGMENTS of Pentecostal or charismatic history which have failed or have achieved only limited success. For one reason or another, they have been slightly out of focus. These examples, however, are the exception rather than the rule, if we consider the longer history of the movement. Overall, the Pentecostals have demonstrated the greatest growth rates of any Christian movement during this century, and therefore deserve — and are receiving — the attention of the church worldwide.

The crucial question, at least in my mind, is whether these movements have contributed significantly to world evangelization. The answer, I believe, is a positive "yes." Perhaps it would be profitable, therefore, to look at several cases of charismatic movements that have experienced great success, in an effort to learn what they may have in common.

William Joseph Seymour (Los Angeles, California)

In my early studies of the development of Pentecostalism, I was impressed with the number of evangelists and missionaries who went out with little or no institutional or financial support, often with only a one-way ticket to their destination. I have dubbed these the "missionaries of the one-way ticket."

The person who first drew my attention to this phenomenon was William Joseph Seymour, pastor of the fabled Azusa Street Mission in Los Angeles, from which Pentecostalism spread around the world. He was born in poverty in rural Louisiana to parents who themselves had been born as slaves.

Seymour migrated as a young man to Indiana, where he worked in several jobs — as a waiter in restaurants and as a porter on the railroad. A deeply religious man, he joined a Methodist Episcopal church in Indianapolis, where he became involved in the holiness movement. Later he joined the "Evening Light Saints," another name for the Church of God, headquartered in Anderson, Indiana.

By 1905, Seymour had moved to Houston, Texas, where he was asked to pastor a small Baptist church with holiness leanings. It was here that he met Charles Fox Parham, who was now teaching a full-blown Pentecostalism in another school. In a short time, Seymour was invited to preach in a small black holiness church in Los Angeles. Accordingly, he was given a one-way ticket by Parham for the journey to California.

The rest of the story is now history. For Seymour, the major factor is that he never bought a return ticket to Houston. For the rest of his life, he lived in Los Angeles and died and was buried there. He served as pastor of the Azusa Street Mission, which sent pilgrims all over the world to spread the Pentecostal flame.

Gaston Barnabas Cashwell (North Carolina)

A similar story can be told about Gaston Barnabas Cashwell, who is often called "the apostle of Pentecost to the South."

Cashwell in 1906 was a minister in the Holiness Church of North Carolina, his native state. A former Methodist, he had preached holiness for nine years before learning about Azusa Street. When he heard about speaking in tongues, he experienced a tremendous hunger for such a baptism in the Holy Spirit. After much agonizing and prayer, he and his wife agreed for him to sell some property in order to buy a one-way railroad ticket to Los Angeles.

Upon arrival at the Azusa Street Mission, Cashwell was dismayed to see it in the control of blacks, and refused to allow hands to be laid on him for the baptism in the Holy Spirit. Later that night, in his hotel room, he suffered a "crucifixion" of his racial pride, and returning to the mission the next night, he requested the laying on of hands by Seymour and other blacks. He immediately spoke in tongues (German, as he claimed).

A few days later, Seymour received an offering for Cashwell which not only paid for a return ticket, but for a new suit of clothes as well. Returning to North Carolina, Cashwell opened a Pentecostal revival in an old tobacco warehouse in Dunn, North Carolina. The revival services lasted for over a month. As a result, much of the southern holiness movement accepted evidential tongues and entered into the ranks of the Pentecostals.

The denominations which joined the movement through Cashwell's ministry were: the Pentecostal Holiness Church, the Pentecostal Free-Will Baptist Church and the Church of God (Cleveland, Tennessee). Indirectly, scores of other groups also were influenced by Cashwell's six-month ministry in 1906-7.

Charles Harrison Mason (Church of God in Christ)

Another pilgrim to Azusa Street was C. H. Mason, who along with C. P. Jones, was a founding father of the predominantly black Church of God in Christ, with headquarters in Memphis, Tennessee. In 1907, hearing of the Azusa Street revival, Mason and two friends traveled to Los Angeles to investigate the baptism in the Holy Spirit and the phenomenon of speaking in tongues. They stayed for several weeks, finally receiving the Pentecostal experience, and returned to Memphis.

Jones, who had not made the pilgrimage, refused to accept the tongues-attested baptism, and a struggle between Mason and Jones ensued. In the end, Mason and the Pentecostal party prevailed, keeping the name and charter of the Church of God in Christ. Jones and his followers then separated to form a non-Pentecostal holiness group, known as the "Church of Christ (Holiness)." In the years since 1908, both churches have gone their separate ways and have evangelized throughout the United States.

The contrasting record of growth between these two churches is of great interest, since both started at about the same time with approximately the same number of members.

By 1990, the Church of Christ (Holiness) claimed 15,000 members in 130 churches in the United States, while the Church of God in Christ claimed 3,700,000 members in 8,000 U.S. congregations. The only theological difference between the two denominations is the importance given to the charismata in the Church of God in Christ. The only other factor which might explain the difference in growth, that I can think of, would be the quality of leadership.

William H. Durham (Chicago, Illinois)

The theological father of the Assemblies of God was William H. Durham, pastor of Chicago's North Avenue Mission. When he saw manifestations of the charismata in his church in 1906, he determined to go to Los Angeles and investigate the Azusa Street revival. In March, 1907, he received the tongues experience under Seymour, who prophesied that wherever Durham preached, "the Holy Spirit would fall upon the people."

Returning to Chicago, Durham led a historic Pentecostal revival where people were often "slain in the Spirit" as they walked in the doors. A "pulpit prodigy," Durham was also an original theologian. Although he was a long-time preacher of Wesleyan holiness, in 1910 he began to teach what he called the "finished work" theory of gradual sanctification, which became the hallmark of the Assemblies of God when it was organized in 1914. Although he died in 1912, Durham's theology exercised a powerful influence on most of the other Pentecostal and charismatic movements that were formed after 1914.

Many leaders and missionaries around the world received their Pentecostal formation under Durham in Chicago. Included among them were E. N. Bell, founder of the Assemblies of God, A. H. Argue, founder of the Pentecostal Assemblies of Canada, Daniel Berg, founder of the Brazilian Assemblies of God, and Luigi Francescon, founder of the

Pentecostal movement of Italy, as well as of Italian Pentecostalism in Brazil and Argentina. Durham's periodical, *The Pentecostal Testimony* was greatly influential in spreading the Pentecostal movement around the world.

Thomas Ball Barratt (Europe)

The apostle of Pentecost to Western Europe was Thomas Ball Barratt, a born Englishman whose family emigrated to Norway in 1867 when he was five years old. A talented musician, he studied music with Edvard Grieg. By 1891, however, he had forsaken a career in music and was ordained an elder in the Norwegian Methodist Church. He soon became active in the Methodist Holiness movement.

In 1906, while on a fund-raising tour in New York City, he heard of the Pentecostal movement emanating from Azusa Street. Like many others at the time, he thought it was necessary to travel to Los Angeles to receive the Pentecostal experience. He was surprised, however, to receive the baptism in the Holy Spirit in his hotel room where he not only spoke but sang arias in other tongues. He immediately returned to Cristiana (Oslo) to open the first Pentecostal meeting in Europe.

Barratt left the Methodist church in 1916 and organized the Filadelfia Church in Oslo, which became a model congregation for the Pentecostals of Scandinavia and Western Europe. He influenced the beginnings of Pentecostalism in Britain, Sweden, Denmark and Germany. His influence on Alexander Boddy in England, Jonathan Paul in Germany and Lewi Pethrus in Sweden helped put his stamp on European Pentecostalism. He lived in his adopted land of Norway and died there in 1940.

Ivan Efimovich Voronaev (Russia)

The missionary of the one-way ticket to Russia and the Slavic nations was a Cossack born in central Russia by the name of Ivan Efimovich Voronaev. Baptized in the Russian Orthodox Church, he was converted in 1908 and became a Baptist pastor. Because of severe persecution in Russia, he emigrated to the United States in 1912, pastoring Russian Baptist churches in San Francisco and New York City.

In 1919, while serving as pastor of the Russian Baptist Church in Manhattan, he came into contact with Pentecostals, and after receiving the tongues-attested baptism, he founded the first Russian Pentecostal Church in New York City. This pastorate was short-lived, however, due to an unusual call to return as a missionary to Russia. Its happened in a cottage prayer meeting where a prophetic utterance changed the course of his life. The words were: "Voronaev, Voronaev, journey to Russia."

As a result of this prophecy, Voronaev and his family journeyed to Russia in the summer of 1920, where he was instrumental in founding the first Russian Pentecostal churches. His later ministry in other Slavic lands resulted in the founding of 350 Pentecostal congregations. In 1929, Voronaev was arrested by the communist authorities and placed in a prison in the Gulag Archipelago.

Voronaev paid the ultimate price — martyrdom — for his faith. Although his wife was released after serving 24 years in Russian prisons, he died somewhere in Siberia and is buried in an unknown grave. As a martyr, Voronaev was the ultimate missionary of the one-way ticket.

Luigi Francescon (Italy, North and South America)

One of the least known but most successful Pentecostal pioneer missionaries was Luigi Francescon, who founded flourishing evangelical-Pentecostal movements among Italians in North and South America, as well as in his native Italy. Born in 1866 in Udine, Italy, Francescon emigrated to the United States at the age of twenty-three. There he found work in Chicago as as mosaic tile-setter. A year later, in an Italian Waldensian service, Francescon was converted from his native Roman Catholicism to the Protestant faith. He then became a member of the First Italian Presbyterian Church of Chicago.

In 1907 he became a Pentecostal through attending William Durham's North Avenue Mission. After Francescon received the baptism in the Holy Spirit, Durham prophesied that he was called of God to the bring the gospel to the Italian people of the world.

In that same year, Francescon and a friend, Pietro Ottolini, established the first American Italian Pentecostal congregation, which he called the "Assemblea Cristiana." Soon afterwards he traveled around the United States and Canada, founding other similar congregations. Many of these churches became the nucleus of the present Christian Church of North America.

Francescon visited Argentina in 1909, establishing the Iglesia Cristiana Pentecostal de Argentina (100,000 members in 1980). The following year he traveled to Brazil, where he founded the Italian Pentecostal movement known as Congregationi Christiani (3,600 churches with 1,000,000 members in 1980).

In 1908 an associate, Giacomo Lombardi, opened the first Pentecostal church in Italy. On subsequent journeys to his native land, Francescon, along with Lombardi, founded congregations among his family and friend. These, after World War II, became known as the Italian Assemblies of God, with 1,000 churches totalling one million members.

Willis Collins Hoover (Chile)

The father of Chilean Pentecostalism was Dr. Willis C. Hoover, a physician turned missionary from Chicago. He went to Chile in 1889 at the age of 33 as a missionary teacher under William Taylor, the pioneering Methodist Holiness missionary bishop. He chose Chile after receiving an inner call that repeatedly said, "South America, South America, South America." Although lacking in theological training, Hoover rose rapidly in the Methodist hierarchy, becoming a district superintendent. He also served as pastor of the First Methodist Church in Valparaiso, which at the time was the largest Methodist church in Chile.

Using the techniques of Wesley's early Methodist societies, Hoover organized class meetings, branch chapels, house-to-house visitation and street preaching to gain converts. Most of his converts were of the poorest working classes. As he began his Valparaiso pastorate, a revival of second-work sanctification swept through the Chilean Methodist churches, similar to the earlier holiness revivals in the United States.

In 1907, Hoover received a book entitled *The Baptism of the Holy Ghost and Fire,* written by Minnie Abrams, a missionary to India. It told of tongues, trances, visions, dreams and other phenomena occurring among widows and orphans in a girls' school in Puna, India, run by Pandita Ramabai.

At about this time, a poor night watchman told Hoover of a vision in which Jesus appeared to him saying, "Go to your pastor and tell him to gather the most spiritual people in the congregation. They are to pray together every day. I intend to baptize them with tongues of fire." After this, a small group gathered daily at the 5:00 P.M. tea time to pray and wait for revival.

In a short time, incredible things began to happen among the Methodists of Chile. They spoke in tongues, danced in the Spirit, experienced spiritual visions and prophesied about a mighty awakening that was about to begin. The churches experienced sudden, spectacular growth in all parts of the nation.

But soon the Methodist authorities held a trial, and on September 12, 1909, expelled 37 members for being "irrational and anti-Methodist." This small group then organized the "Pentecostal Methodist Church of Chile." Hoover told them to preach in the streets every Sunday, and that "Chile sera para Cristo" ("Chile shall belong to Christ.") How well they planted churches across the nation is seen in the popular saying that in every village throughout Chile there is sure to be a post office and a Pentecostal Methodist church.

The results have been astounding. Despite incredible persecutions from both Protestants and Catholics, the Pentecostals have grown to be by far the largest non-Catholic denomination in Chile. The "Catedral Evangelica" in Santiago has been expanded to seat 15,000 persons, with a choir and orchestra of 4,000 members. This church, along with its "annexes," numbered no less than 350,000 adherents in 1990. The total number of Pentecostals in Chile now is approaching the two million mark, 20 percent of the population of the nation.

Hoover was truly a missionary of the one-way ticket. He became a Chilean citizen. He incorporated Chilean criollo music in his church services. He lived, died (in 1936), and was buried in his adopted land. The movement he left behind has changed the religious and even the political landscape of Chile forever.

Daniel Berg and Gunnar Vingren (Brazil)

Perhaps the most striking story of these missionaries of the one-way ticket is that of Daniel Berg and Gunnar Vingren, the apostles of Brazilian Pentecostalism. These two men were young immigrants from Sweden who had settled in South Bend, Indiana, in 1902. In Sweden they had already been converted as Baptists and came to the United States because of an economic depression in their native land. In 1909, they were baptized in the Holy Spirit, although they continued to attend Baptist churches.

In 1910, Vingren accepted the pastorate of a Swedish Baptist Church in South Bend. It was there that the two men heard a prophetic utterance which repeated the word "Para." An interpretation of the word was given which directed both Berg and Vingren to go somewhere in the world called "Para." Since no one in the group had any idea where such a place might be, Berg and Vingren visited the Chicago Public Library, where a search of a World Almanac revealed that there was indeed a province in Northeastern Brazil called "Pará" on the Pará River.

They immediately made plans to go to Brazil, with offerings collected by friends sufficient to buy two one-way tickets to Belém, capital of the province of Pará. On their way to New York, however, they stopped at a Pentecostal mission in Pittsburgh, and in response to a financial appeal, gave all their money in the offering. The next day, as they walked the streets praying about their dilemma, a totally unknown woman came to them and gave them the exact amount to get to New York and to purchase one-way tickets to Belém in a tramp steamer. They had never seen the woman before.

They arrived in Brazil in November of 1910 and began

preparations for a missionary ministry. Berg worked as a cob-
bler and in a shipping company while Vingren studied Portuguese. Together they attended a Baptist church while they
learned the language. Shortly, through their ministry, many
Baptists received the Pentecostal experience, after which
tongues, interpretations, prophecies and healings began to
occur in the services.

The pastor then forbade these manifestations in the
sanctuary, but allowed the Swedes to have Pentecostal meetings in the church basement. Soon everyone was in the basement. Thus began the first Pentecostal congregation in Brazil
which was organized in 1911 with only 18 members. They
called their denomination the "Assembleias de Deus" (Assemblies of God) of Brazil and began to plant churches all over the
nation.

The growth of Pentecostalism in Brazil has been nothing
less than phenomenal. Brazil now has at one and the same
time the largest Catholic and largest Pentecostal populations
of any nation on earth. They are the only two churches with
congregations in every province and important city in Brazil.
As William Read said about the Pentecostals, "In every town,
Singer sewing machines, Coca Cola, Lucky Strike and the
Assemblies are there." At the last count, the Pentecostals of
Brazil claimed over 15 million members, more than the number of Southern Baptists in the United States.

Although Vingren died in 1932, Berg was able to attend
the fiftieth anniversary celebration of the Assemblies of God in
Brazil in 1961. At that time the church he had founded half a
century before numbered over 1,000,000 members. (This can
be contrasted with John Wesley, who had 100,000 Methodist
followers at the time of his death.)

The missionaries of the one-way ticket in the early part
of this twentieth century were the human instruments of the
Christian church's most phenomenal expansion in history.
They obeyed the Holy Spirit.

Back door departures

EVERY MOVEMENT OF ANY KIND HAS ITS DROPOUTS and backsliders. This has been true, of course, of the Pentecostals and charismatics. In fact, the history of these movements is replete with well-known dropouts from the earliest days. The high energy and emotional levels of early Pentecostalism no doubt caused many who preferred "blessed quietness" to move on to more traditional churches.

When David Barrett produced his landmark survey in 1988, he included two never-before-seen categories which he called "post-Pentecostals" and "post-charismatics," terms which raised eyebrows among Pentecostals and Pentecostal-watchers. What did these labels mean? Who were they? Just how many of them were there?

In my own experience, I have known hundreds of Pentecostals who have become Baptists, or Methodists, etc., for various reasons. Among charismatics, my most vivid memory was one of the first Catholic charismatics I met when I spoke for the first time at Notre Dame in 1972. As we shared a taxi ride to the campus, I was impressed with his joy and enthusiasm. His example helped me form a positive attitude towards the whole Catholic and Protestant renewal.

About fifteen years later, I accidently passed him in an airport, and ran over to greet him, hoping to renew our acquaintance. To my surprise, he absolutely would not discuss his charismatic experiences and abruptly called off the conversation. Obviously, something traumatic had happened to him in the intervening years. He was a "post-charismatic."

The following two definitions by Barrett would be helpful at this point.

Post-Pentecostals: former members of Pentecostal denominations who have left to join non-pentecostal denominations (due to marriage, family moves, job transfers, upward mobility, new interest in liturgy and theology, et. al.), but who have not renounced their Pentecostal experience, and still identify themselves as Pentecostal.

Post-charismatics: Self-identified charismatics within mainline non-Pentecostal denominations who are no longer regularly active in the charismatic movement but have moved into other spheres of witness and service in their churches.

In both cases, post-charismatics are distinguished from active charismatics in that they no longer attend regular weekly or monthly meetings that are specifically charismatic in nature.

Post-Pentecostals

In helping Barrett prepare his survey, I gave him information on the church of which I have been a lifetime member, the Pentecostal Holiness Church. According to my estimates, the former members of the church are three times the number of their current membership. (Barrett places the figures at 450,000 post and 150,000 current in the U.S.) Three-fourths of the people leave by the back door.

Now this is not altogether bad, as we have already seen. Many —perhaps most — of the former Pentecostals are active elsewhere in the Christian community.

Among the millions of post-Pentecostals are some well known American church leaders, including the president of Fuller Theological Seminary, David Hubbard, whose roots go back to his parents' Pentecostal ministry in California. Thomas Wang, former head of the Lausanne movement, attended the Assemblies of God Bible School in Springfield as a young man, while Tom Houston, his successor, has spiritual roots among Anglican charismatics. Only time will tell if the new Archbishop of Canterbury, George Carey, will continue to be an active charismatic or will join the ranks of the post-charismatics.

Other famous names that immediately come to mind are Oral Roberts, now a Methodist, and Charles Stanley, pastor of the First Baptist Church of Atlanta, both of whom were born and raised in the Pentecostal Holiness Church. In my own home town of Oklahoma City, the pastors of the First Baptist Church, Charles Garrison, and of the First Methodist Church, Nick Harris, come from Assemblies of God backgrounds.

I recently came across a book by a post-Pentecostal who left the Pentecostal Holiness Church to join the Seventh-Day Adventists. Called *Praise the Lord: A Pentecostal Preacher Looks for Light*, the book chronicles the pilgrimage of its author, James Beshires, from Pentecostalism to Adventism.

This would not surprise you so much if you were to read a tract which was handed to me last summer on the sidewalk in Indianapolis. Quite by chance, I found myself in the General Conference of the Seventh Day Adventist Church. It was in session at the Hoosier Dome. I wanted to see what the convention hall was like, because we were coming in a couple of weeks later. So I walked in to discover 40,000 Adventists in their annual meeting.

On the sidewalk outside, a man handed me a tract entitled "Seventh Day Adventist Churches Turning to Pentecostalism." And was I interested! I grabbed it and said to the man,"What does this mean?" He didn't know who I was, of course.

"It's terrible," he replied. "Seventh Day Adventists are speaking with tongues. They raise their hands. They use overhead projectors, and sing Scripture choruses. It's awful!"

"Really?" I responded. "You know, that sounds wonderful to me!"

"What?" he came back.

I told him who I was, the chairman of the congress meeting there in a few weeks. And I read his tract about the new trends among the Adventists. Their congregations are called "celebration churches" and they're starting up in Oregon and California. They're huge churches and growing like crazy. Furthermore, the tract said that other Adventist leaders are approving them and sending pastors to these churches to learn how to do it.

"I guess you can speak in tongues on Saturday as well as on Sunday, if you want to," I told the sidewalk propagandist as I took my leave.

Some post-Pentecostals have recently been making the pilgrimage to Eastern Orthodoxy. One interesting case is that of Dr. Andrew Walker, director of the C. S. Lewis Centre in London. Coming from the Elim Pentecostal Church of Britain, he is now a lay theologian and preacher in the Russian Orthodox Church. I was told about Walker by Karen Jermyn, director of the Holy Ghost Research Center at Oral Roberts University, who herself recently made the change from the Assemblies of God to the Greek Orthodox Church.

A rare event is when an entire Pentecostal congregation joins a mainline Protestant denomination as a body. A well publicized case was that of the Church of the King Episcopal Church in Valdosta, Georgia, which was organized in 1990. Established by Stan White, a former minister of the Assemblies of God, the church was formed from a split in the large Evangel Assembly of God Church in Valdosta, which was pastored by White's father, James White.

Attracted by the liturgical tradition represented by the Episcopal Church, Stan White led his followers into the church with high profile publicity in *Christianity Today*, which gave major coverage in a lead article entitled "Why the Bishops Went to Valdosta." In spite of the new congregation's "southern-fried liturgy," which included all the enthusiastic spontaneity of a charismatic prayer meeting, the churches of the diocese were unanimous in welcoming the new congregation.

According to White, he "envisions a church that is fully charismatic, fully evangelical, but also fully liturgical and sacramental." Apparently, this new congregation would be classified as "post-Pentecostal," but still actively charismatic.

The crossover, however, is not a one-way street.

There are millions of "post-Methodists," "post-Baptists," "post-Presbyterians," and "post-Catholics," etc., who have become Pentecostals in the past several years. The latest estimate is that no less than 100,000 independent charismatic congregations have been planted in the United States alone since World War II, mainly by crossovers from mainline churches.

The point is that there has always been a great deal of church changing in American religious life that goes in every direction. One suspects, moreover, that if all the "post-Pentecostals" were removed from Methodist pulpits in America, the American Methodist Church would be in a major crisis indeed. Eighty percent of the Asbury (Seminary) student body are said to be charismatic.

The worldwide number of post-Pentecostals worldwide in 1990 was placed at only 3,000,000 by Barrett, far fewer than I would have guessed.

Post-charismatics

Barrett has commented on the "enormous turnover" among denominational charismatics, both Protestant and Catholic. Among Lutherans, for example, the number of first-time participants in the Minneapolis conferences has consistently been at or near 25 percent. This implies an average four-year turnover rate. For American Catholics the rate is much greater — an average two to three-year turnover rate.

The 1990 figures for Protestants and Catholics in the United States are revealing:

Active Protestant charismatics	23,722,050
Post-charismatic Protestants	31,600,000
Active Catholic charismatics	11,813,000
Post-charismatic Catholics	60,250,000

For many years, the large number of post-charismatics has been a continuing concern, especially for Catholic charismatic leaders. Some bishops are becoming increasingly worried about the large numbers of Catholics who are leaving the Church to join what they call the "fundamentalist sects." The problem of hemorrhage is especially severe in Latin America and the Philippines. An estimated 200,000 Catholics leave the church annually in Manila alone. Many of these are post-charismatic Catholics who become active Pentecostals.

Several years ago, Catholic leaders spoke frequently of the "alumni" or "graduates" of the movement who have gone on to serve the Lord and the church in various ministries. It is generally acknowledged by them that most of their Christian education directors, Sunday school teachers and other volunteers in the Catholic churches now come from charismatic backgrounds. The large majority of lay ministers have charismatic roots.

Recently, however, many are talking about the "plateau-ing" or decline of the renewal movement. Latterly, the attendance at major Catholic charismatic conferences, such as the bellwether annual meeting at Notre Dame, has apparently fallen. The Notre Dame gathering has receded from a high of 33,000 in 1973 to an average of 8,000 for the past several years. Leaders explain, however, that in the early days, Notre Dame was the only such large charismatic conference. Now there are no less than 45 regional annual conferences which together attract more than the early Notre Dame meetings. Furthermore, the existence of Catholic charismatics is no longer newsworthy. And as a positive sign, Director Bill Beatty of the National Service Committee points to a great growth in the number of prayer groups in the U.S., now numbering more than 6,000.

Record growth and huge conferences in Third World countries reflect a continued explosive expansion for the movement worldwide. Overseas, it is absolutely booming. For instance, the 1989 national meeting in Italy drew 50,000 to the congress in Turin. It is also estimated that there are no less than 350,000 Catholic charismatics in Korea.

Despite this evidence of growth, some leaders are bemoaning the future with headlines such as the following from Charles Whitehead: "Is it all over for the Charismatic Renewal?" Whitehead is the new executive of the International Catholic Charismatic Renewal Office (ICCRO) in Rome. His concern was echoed by Ralph Martin in a major address at the Indianapolis Congress in August, 1990.

It should be remembered, however, that the renewal movement is only 30 years old — and barely 23, among Catholics. The future is still unpredictable. Only time will tell.

"Surf's up!" — The Third Wave

WHEN I FIRST HEARD THE TERM "THIRD WAVE," I was struck by the repeated use of the word "third" in the history of the Pentecostal movement.

Of course, Pentecostalism strongly stresses the person and work of the Third Person of the Trinity. And in the 1950's the movement was perceived as a new and third stream. Although Lesslie Newbigin in his 1953 book, *The Household of God*, was the first to recognize this, it was given major definition as a "third force" in Christendom, alongside Protestantism and Catholicism, by Henry Van Dusen in a 1958 article in *Life* magazine.

Also in the 1950's, a Roman Catholic scholar in Chile by the name of Vergara wrote a book called *Tongues of Fire*. It spoke of "three reformations" in Chile: (1) the Protestant, (2) the Wesleyan, and (3) the Pentecostal reformations.

In the United States, after the outbreak of Pentecostalism in the mainline Protestant churches in 1960 and in the Roman Catholic Church in 1967, Ralph Martin popularized the "Three Stream" approach within Pentecostalism, which recognized the "classical Pentecostals," the "Protestant charismatics," and the "Catholic charismatics." The subsequent Kansas City conference was organized by leaders from these "three streams." By the time the New Orleans Congress (1987) and the Indianapolis Congress (1990) were organized, a "four streams" approach was used, which recognized the many and vast nondenominational movements as a major stream in their own right.

In the meantime, a new penetration began among

mainline evangelicals, primarily through the influence of Peter Wagner and John Wimber at Fuller Theological Seminary. A focus of this development was Wimber's controversial "Signs, Wonders and Church Growth" class at Fuller. Widely publicized by Robert Walker in *Christian Life* magazine (reprinted by the "hundreds of thousands of copies"), these classes opened the door for thousands of evangelical pastors to receive charismatic experiences outside the context of Pentecostal or charismatic circles.

By 1983, Peter Wagner had presented a new configuration by using the term "Third Wave" to refer to "straightline evangelicals and other Christians" who are "open to the supernatural work of the Holy Spirit that the Pentecostals and charismatics have experienced, but without becoming either charismatic or Pentecostal." Indeed, Wagner saw himself in just such terms.

> *I see myself as neither a charismatic nor a Pentecostal. I belong to the Lake Avenue Congregational Church. I'm a Congregationalist. My church is not a charismatic church, although some of our members are charismatic.... However, our church is more and more open to the same way that the Holy Spirit does work among charismatics. For example, our pastor gives an invitation after every service .... for people who need physical healing or inner healing to come forward and go to the prayer room and be anointed with oil and prayed for, and we have teams of people who know how to pray for the sick.*

> *We like to think that we are doing it in a congregational way: we are not doing it in a charismatic way. But we're getting the same results. I myself have several major theological differences with Pentecostals and charismatics, which don't mar any kind of mutual ministry, but keep me from saying I'm a charismatic.[1]*

---

1   Wagner, Peter, "A Third Wave?" *Pastoral Renewal*, July-August 1983.

These differences, he explained later in an article which appeared in the May-June 1988 issue of *AD2000:*

> *"The Third Wave" by Peter Wagner takes the position that the baptism of the Holy Spirit occurs at conversion and is not to be sought as a separate work of grace ... Third Wavers ... affirm speaking in other tongues, but simply as one of many other gifts of the Spirit which God distributes to different members of the Body of Christ .... Experientially, the principal glue which binds Pentecostals and charismatics together is that they testify to having had 'the experience' of 'the baptism' ... no such experience characterizes the Third Wave...*

Evidently this explanation accurately describes the experience of multitudes of people all over the world. Barrett now classifies the Pentecostal-charismatic tendency as: (1) classical Pentecostalism, (2) the charismatic renewal movement, both Catholic and Protestant, and (3) the Third Wave. According to him, there are no less than 33,000,000 people worldwide who would be more comfortable with the Third Wave classification than with any other. As an indication, at the Indianapolis Congress in August of 1990, some Southern Baptist and Church of Christ leaders conducted a "Third Wave" conference which attracted overflow crowds and drew no criticism.

Criticisms of the Third Wave

The idea of a "Third Wave," while seen by many classical Pentecostals as a wonderful new way of expanding the ranks of Pentecostalism, is finding some determined resistance from some older "neo-Pentecostals" who generally support the necessity of tongues as the consequence of a post-conversion experience of "baptism in the Holy Spirit."

In 1989, Dennis Bennett, whose 1959 tongues experience marked the beginning of "neo-Pentecostalism" in the mainline churches, complained about the concept of a "Third Wave" because in it he saw the seeds of the destruction of the charismatic renewal. To Bennett, Wagner's position was a "modified evangelical position that clearly leaves out the very essence and meaning of Pentecost." Although he acknowledges that "it is the most open stance the evangelicals have taken thus far," he maintains that "it is not far enough for those of us who have already entered in, and know the blessings they are not yet accepting."

In an article in his newsletter, entitled "The Old Paths," Bennett warned against the Third Wave because "God's Spirit does not come in waves," since we serve an "unwavering God." He further says, "Waves are beautiful, but they wash things away." To Bennett the greatest concern was that the acceptance of Third Wave theology "would allow preachers and priests all over town to breathe a sigh of relief, since they need no longer seek a definite experience of baptism in the Holy Spirit."

In summary, Bennett explained his conception of what Third Wave evangelicals were really saying: "If you good people would just stop insisting that there is a baptism in the Holy Spirit following salvation, and that it is important to speak in tongues, we will all get along fine."

Bennett is afraid of a diffused movement without a focal point of experience. But in my own travels I meet increasing numbers of people who find the "Third Wave" idea to be an attractive way to describe their situation. I suspect that there are thousands of denominational churches — like the Southern Baptist Church in Oklahoma City — that appear to be completely charismatic in worship, but would strongly deny that they are Pentecostal or charismatic.

Moving towards A.D. 2000

This may point to a very important development in Pentecostal relations with evangelicals in the last few decades. Russell Spittler referred to this in Harold Smith's recent book, *Pentecostals from the Inside Out*. He maintains that from the end of World War II to the end of the Vietnam era, America saw the "evangelicalization of the Pentecostals" through their relationship with the National Association of Evangelicals and the National Religious Broadcasters. Since the close of the Vietnam War, Spittler suggests a period of the "Pentecostalization of the evangelicals." That is quite an important reality.

This was dramatically illustrated in the Lausanne II conference in Manila in 1989, where Pentecostals and charismatics made up from one third to one half of all the participants. At times, the services appeared to be charismatic rallies. The "Holy Spirit track" drew by far the largest attendance of any workshop presented in the congress.

The evening service shared by J. I. Packer and Jack Hayford was for many a highlight of the conference, and quite possibly a watershed in evangelical history. Hayford's sermon, "A Passion for Fullness," (in which he suggested the broad label "pleromatics", derived from the Greek word for "fullness," to cover both segments) was a well-received plea for evangelicals to move into a full experience of the Holy Spirit, where signs and wonders would spark a worldwide evangelistic explosion.

The New Orleans and Indianapolis congresses on "The Holy Spirit and World Evangelization," held in 1987 and 1990, represented an awakening of all North American Pentecostals and charismatics to enter a "decade of world evangelization" which would end with a great worldwide celebration in the year A.D. 2000. The announced goal has been unabashed and ambitious: "to win a majority of the human race to Jesus Christ by the year A.D. 2000."

Roman Catholics are also catching the vision for world evangelization. The vision of a Christian majority by A.D. 2000 was originally announced by Tom Forrest, a Redemptorist priest long active in the charismatic renewal. In September of 1990, he led over 5,000 priests in an evangelization retreat in the Vatican which called all Catholics to join in a decade of evangelization. It had the full backing of Pope John Paul II, who now speaks of the Roman Catholic Church as "the Church of the New Evangelization."

Perhaps the ultimate purpose of the Pentecostal-charismatic renewal movements is to bring the signs-and-wonders gifts of the Holy Spirit back to the church in order to lead the way for the most intensive and successful period of evangelization in the history of the Faith.

The Lord is trying, I believe, to call all of us together to evangelize the world — to make Christ's kingdom come, and his will be done, "on earth as it is in heaven."